Frances Matthews, is an ordinary 52-year-old woman. She was born in a small town in Oxfordshire, into a loving family, whose life began just like anyone else's. She started work at 16 and married at 25. She then suffered a life-threatening illness, eight days after marrying. She had two daughters, and two granddaughters; went through a double sudden loss of parents, followed by a divorce after 30 years.

She embarked on a new relationship, and had written this true story on what turned out to be a personal, almost fatal relationship that went terribly wrong. She is now on the long road to rehabilitation.

This book is dedicated to my sisters Kim, Sam, Josh, Nathan, Jess; and friends Lisa, Lydia and Jackie. To those who would survive, and those who sadly do not.

Frances Matthews

A GLIMMER OF HOPE

AUSTIN MACAULEY PUBLISHERS™

LONDON • CAMBRIDGE • NEW YORK • SHARJAH

A CIP catalogue record for this title is available from the British Library.

ISBN 9781398424715 (Paperback)
ISBN 9781398424722 (ePub e-book)

www.austinmacauley.com

First Published 2022
Austin Macauley Publishers Ltd®
1 Canada Square
Canary Wharf
London
E14 5AA

Metropolitan Police, the detectives of the Domestic Unit (London), CPS, Crown Court Services, Witness Service, Headway, CAB, Social Services, Therapeutic Counsellors, Freedom Course, The Volunteering Charity Services.

I met James in July of 2015 on the dating app 'Plenty of Fish'. I had met a few 'meets' off there; one or two were okay, the others not so good, but friends had said don't let a couple put you off. I didn't. James started chatting to me. I always thought of myself as opened-minded. But blimey, I didn't expect the kinds of chat I was getting from quite a lot of men, but James came across as a cheeky chappie; we chatted for many hours on the phone discussing life, childhood, music, work, all kinds of things. He made me feel comfortable.

He kept on about meeting up as I was only a 30-minute drive away, but I made him wait for about four weeks, then we arranged to meet. I would be driving to meet him at his place of work. I was nervous on my way there, I hadn't been on the dating scene for years, I made sure I told him I wasn't a size 10. I was a size 18 with curves, he seemed really keen. Then I was on my way there as I had spoken to James just before leaving, he said if he liked me, he would take me out the back and show me his dart board!

Before I knew it, I had driven past his place of work. He had seen me and rang me as we were both laughing as he thought I had seen him and carried on. I parked up and he introduced himself and kissed me on the cheek. He took me into his place of work, made me a cup of coffee and that was it, we started dating. I had told him a lot about my life, my family and friends, I was going through a divorce and over time opened up more to him, telling him about losing both of my parents eight months apart. I was still emotional about it. I absolutely loved my mum and dad, the best parents ever!!! He listened, and I couldn't believe his understanding; he was affectionate, caring and very charming. It took me time to accept this showing of affection as I wasn't shown this in my marriage, it was alien to me.

We went out for meals, drinks. He introduced me to work colleagues and his friends, then he surprised me by wanting me to meet his mum at which I thought, *Gosh, this is going well, really well*. I met his mum, we got on great, things were going good but a year into our relationship, I received a message from this woman. I didn't knew her. *Why is this woman messaging me?*

I read it, James was having an affair with her; an old school friend. I was heartbroken, he said he loved me, I felt a fool, a total fool. I rang him, he couldn't stop apologising, but wasn't happy as this happened on his birthday; he was blaming me. *What had I done?*

I just got into my car, and drove and drove, and smoked cigarette one after another. I ended up back at the house we were sharing with one other and locked myself in. We spoke later in the day; him saying sorry, he loved me and chose me not her. *Wasn't I enough for him?* I thought our relationship was going good; this was a total shock to me but we worked it out. I said to him he had a lot to prove to me, especially trust. Our relationship carried on but I started to see a slight change to him, he didn't like it if his friends spoke to me especially men, even if a stranger smiled at me, or even said good morning, he didn't like it. He would moan; I just kept thinking where had this gentleman gone, this caring and charming man.

Everything came to a head at Christmas 2016. I decided to leave for my older sister, paid for my taxi back, left him a letter explaining. My God, did I got abusive emails!!! I got those over a few days, and over the weeks his emails got kinder... The gentleman that I met at the beginning was back, I didn't realised at the time what he was doing, I just didn't catch on.

But he was saying I wasn't being looked after, he was worried about me and we had started to get on really well again, like it was in the beginning. I started to visit only at weekends as friends, but he wanted more... He hated me going on a Sunday evening, kept telling me that he missed me and he would look after me. This carried on for a few months until I went back to him, he was over the moon, told me he was my knight in shining armour, didn't everyone deserved a second chance?

Then three months later, he said there was nothing there for us, he wanted me to move to London with him, to look after his mum and granddad. He kept telling me that he was the only one who cared for me and no one else did, I still didn't catch on to what he was doing. I moved to London with him in June 2017... that was when everything changed. He changed. Gone was the caring, understanding, charming and affectionate man I knew, instead in front of me was a man I didn't knew...

The violence started in September; all I did was question why he was in such a foul mood, next minute I was on the floor, hurt with the force that he used. He had got the dressing gown belt so tight around my throat, his hand over my mouth,

I couldn't breathe. I started to panic, I still couldn't breathe, I tried to get his hand off my mouth, I'm tried to push his arm away and suddenly I took in the deepest breath I could. My breath was deep and fast and he then said this was my fault, all of a sudden, he called me a slag; I'm a slut, a retard. *I didn't understood what had I done, had I missed something?*

He told me to get ready, we're going to visit his mum, I looked in the mirror I had marks on my face, bruised lips, I was in shock. I couldn't believe this had happened. I came back into the room when he saw my face, he asked, "Did I do that?"

I replied, "Yes, you did."

He told me, "Cover it up with make-up." I did as I was told. He said he could still see marks, how much more make up could I apply? I didn't said anything but all the time we were with his mum, I kept my head down as much as possible, my face at different angle hoping no one notices. The violence would start again, I didn't even had to say anything, if I used a tone as he said, and if my body shows attitude, I got hit, I was hit so many times I lose count.

One night I answered him back. I was sat on the sofa with my back to him, without warning I'm covered in (soda)pop and it was freezing. Then he slapped me across the face a few times. I tried to protect myself but I was not strong enough. I was pushed onto the sofa and banged my head on the wall. *Hopefully someone heard it?* There was a knock on a door and it was our house sharer, Robert, and he was asking for silence, no one was helping me that day. James told him to mind his own business, it was 'personal', I then got a torrid of abuse, 'I'm a shit mother', 'my daughters didn't loved me', 'my mum and dad would be ashamed of me', 'I'm adopted', 'I'm useless', 'my ex-husband never loved me'. If nothing, the mental abuse was as bad as the violence.

He would keep on like this for hours not minutes, if I answer back, he was worse. I got other liquids poured over me too, water, alcohol, tea, coffee, laundry liquid, t-cut, and fish sauce. God, I hated that it left my body sticky, my hair matted, unless he gave me permission to shower, I stayed like that all night, no questions asked. He said all the time that I wasn't to question him in any way, I knew the consequences. He was nice as pie to me in front of his family but behind closed doors he was Jekyll and Hyde, he got worse. He accused me of having affairs with every man, including neighbours; I wasn't to speak to anyone, he was with me 24/7. He would come to the bathroom with me, he accused me of hiding a phone in the bathroom and kitchen; he timed me for toileting and showering otherwise he had been banging on the door threatening to smash the door. He would place cleaning products on the floor in the bathroom, certain ways, bath sponges, he had put at each side of the bath panel, he said I was hiding a phone, he did this all the time.

Just after Christmas, the new year of 2017, it was February, he started the day accusing me of affairs, I wasn't affectionate enough, I was a waste of time; this went on all day, he was relentless. He would always close the windows so no one outside could see here. It didn't matter what I did, it wasn't enough, he criticized anything I did, making a coffee: he would always say that you didn't make it with love, I wasn't trying enough. I spent the night on the sofa, hoping he would stop. I always tried to block him out but it was impossible, most of the time I cried myself to sleep, sobbing, praying for it to stop. I must had fell asleep, woke up in the morning, him demanding coffee, again drink wasn't good enough, he started again calling me a slut, slag and cunt, I was called that daily, I hated that word. He said I had had all these cocks since being here, something inside me had enough, I replied he had probably had other women, he accused me of having caught something, I replied to him he was the one who had caught something. I knew the moment I said that I was in trouble, the look on his face said it all. Before I knew it, he was on top of me, his legs pinning my arms at my side, then the violence. He hit me so hard across my face, hitting each side of my face, hitting, hitting, hitting, I screamed out, "stop", all I could see was black, I swear I was seeing stars. He got off of me, I couldn't move to begin with, God, my head hurt, I try sitting up but it took me a few attempts, I felt sick, I could taste something I spit in my hand it was blood, I tried to stand, I couldn't, I felt so dizzy, I leaned my head back, I tried to lay down, it felt worse. I sat up again, I was hurting, my head, my whole body, I tried to walk, but I was so unsteady, I sat back down, all he said was, it was my fault!!

He wanted ciggies from the shop, he told me to go and to be back in ten minutes. The shop was a couple of minutes' walk, I walked down the stairs holding on I felt so light headed, I used the walls going to steady myself, I walked into the shop, I didn't even noticed people as I was standing in the queue, the security guard came up to me asking who had done this to my face, I hadn't even looked or knew what I looked like. He asked is it him who is with you all the time, I said yes, he told me to get away, I told him he doesn't understand, he would kill me if I leave him. James said that from when the violence started, if I ever left him, he would make it his life's worth to find me and kill me, including my two daughters. He would say how he would kill me, strangle me, tie me to the bed, he would hang himself above me, also he would put me in the freezer, he could still had my money. I couldn't let him harm my daughters, I couldn't let that happen. I said to this man he didn't understand, I started crying, I said to him I had to go, he would come looking for me. I left, trying to dry my eyes hoping he wouldn't see I had been crying. When I got back, he started on about how people would now look at him as a woman beater, I didn't answer, I was aching still, my head hurt. I went to the bathroom, oh, God, I saw my face in the mirror: I had two black eyes, a big lump, and bruising on the left side of my forehead, my lip is split, bruising on my chin, and all over my chest, I tried not to cry. As I entered the room, he said, "Did I do that?" I replied once again,

"Yes." He said,

"I bruise easily." I felt tired, I went to sit on the sofa, he demanded that I sit next to him on the bed, and said I sleep next to him tonight, so he could look after me. Inside, I didn't wanted to be near him, I had no choice, I knew what would happen if I refuse. I laid down, I eventually drift off. In the morning, I was still aching, I go into the bathroom, my bruises were worse, my black eyes, everything, I looked awful; I looked like a panda, my right eye is bloodshot. He wouldn't let me out, we didn't, for ten days I was in the room with him, he tried to be nice, but kept saying I bruise easily, it was my fault he was a woman beater, I felt nothing. He went to the shop, but locked me in, I couldn't get out. He made excuses to his family that why we hadn't been around. After ten days, he send me to the shop, I still had black eyes, you know that yellow and light purple colour. I walk with my head down, I sensed people were looking at me, as I passed. Three workmen asked if I'm alright, I didn't answered as I could feel the tears in my eyes, I dare not speak to anyone, I knew I would start crying. The beatings continue, the mental abuse was getting worse.

It was on my birthday, I had been to the doctor and spoken briefly about what was happening to me; she gave me a number to ring, victim's abuse. I told her I couldn't take it, because he goes through my bag, and pats me down. Yes, every day he goes through my handbag, pats me down and goes through all my clothes checking for a phone, anything he thinks I'm hiding. In the end, I took the small piece of paper, folded it, I put it under the sponge in my eye makeup console and into my makeup bag. In the evening he started again accusing me of affairs, he didn't trust me; I was a slag, slut. Next minute he had got my handbag, and tipped everything out. I was panicking, he opened up everything, God, no; he found it, demanding to know what it is. I saw the anger in his eyes and face, I told him it was for counselling for couples, he replied, I would be ringing it in the morning, if you're lying to me, you know the consequences. He woke me up, I knew it took me ages to fall asleep, he had rang the number, he knew it was for victim abuse, he shouted at me saying he was the victim not me, I treated him like shit. The next minute, he tied my wrists together with cable ties, it hurt, he slapped me across the face, told me I'm a lying cunt, I need the bathroom, he took pulling me, dragged me back to the room, pushed me onto the bed. Next minute he came in with a saucepan, if you need to piss, he said you go in there or wet yourself, and pushed the sofa next to the door, he made me eat with my wrists tied, I was not hungry, he said if I didn't, he would feed me. The ties hurt bad, bruised around my wrists and as I was trying to make it easier, I made it worse, they got tighter, when he saw my wrists, he took them off, but I was not allowed off the bed. I had to lie next to him, my wrists was hurt, really hurt. He said I was a baby, I didn't sleep well and I didn't drink so I didn't had to wee.

That was my birthday that what he said I deserved. He didn't stop I never knew what he expected daily. He changed the rules, I woke up I wanted to die, I didn't wanted to live anymore, I would rather die than beaten daily, being told what a worthless, useless human being I was, I wanted to be at peace, with my mum and dad, to be with them, I felt nothing, I didn't wanted to live, no more. I knew I would be safe with them. I had a doctor's appointment to get my medication, inhalers, blood pressure tablets. I went for a shower, I got dressed, as I opened the door, he stood there. Before I knew it, he was dragging me by my collar, bellowing, come with me, he accused me of hiding a phone, I told him I hadn't got a phone, he was shouting he didn't believed me, he put a trap out of wires, because they moved I would got them. I had no idea what he was on about, I pleaded with him I hadn't got one, he said if I didn't come up with the phone by midnight, he would choke me, I started crying, I hadn't got a phone, honest, I knew he would choke me. I started crying, sobbing, I was so scared, I knew he would, he strangled me a lot, I was absolutely terrified, he started throwing everything about, clothes, shoes, cutlery, furniture until the whole room was covered, you couldn't see the flooring, the mess was shocking. Then he poured a bottle of coke over me, lucozade, water and the fish sauce I hated. I sat there and cried, he cuddled me. I didn't wanted him near me, I couldn't flinch as I had done that so many times. He had always threatened me and said he would give me something to flinch about if I did it anymore, he said I had to be remorseful? For what, I didn't understand what I did? I had to change. He said, he said, he loved me? That isn't love, I was so scared of him. I noticed I was losing weight, he was putting it on, I was getting thinner than I had ever been in my life. I started to worry, I could feel a lump, the top of my right breast bone, I tried telling him, he was not interested, he said it was my age, I continued to worry, the abuse continued, it was getting worse, I got hit daily, for anything, not looking at him, if I had a tone or attitude, if I questioned him and answered back.

One day we took his aunt and uncle to the retail park, all he did was moan at me the whole time we were out, saying I was a user and a slag. Yes, he was saying this as we were going around the store. I answered him back, told him he was a user, all of a sudden, he turned around and hit me hard across the face. I looked around, his aunt saw him, I could tell by her face, I felt nothing, I just wanted to go. I stood there the next minute his aunt was by my side, "My God, did he do this too you often." I said

"Yes." in a whisper. I said, "Be careful, if he thinks I'm telling you anything, I would get the beating of my life." She stuck by me until we left to go back to their house. She asked James to help his uncle, his aunt and I were left alone, I only had a few minutes. She asked, "Did he do this a lot?" I told her,

"Yes." Before I knew it, everything was rolling off my tongue, I told her he was with me 24/7, he didn't allowed me to speak to my sister. You see, James had already changed the sim for the fourth time, each time he deleted my family and friends. He also smashed my iPhone 7, the night before we left for London, I lost all contact of family and friends. I told her he didn't leave me on my own, he was with me all the time. I showed her all my bruises, across my chest from left to right and the tops of both my legs, as I drop my dress, he walked in, bloody hell that was close. She gave me this smile, a worrying smile; a few minutes later we left. I never saw them again, he would always do that, we stopped going to his cousins, his mum, we just stopped going, you see. I got on with his cousin too, she was very kind to me, but even she noticed how he treated me, he insisted I went shopping with his mum and cousin, he reminded me again about his ability to kill, over time. While in London he told me things he hadn't told me before, he was confessing to me but why, he had killed small animals, he put a frog in a jar in the microwave, I couldn't understand why? Who would do such a thing, and when he was in his twenties, he had brought a crossbow and shot an arrow into a pigeon that luckily had flown away with the arrow still in its wing, but he shot a squirrel dead, I sat there thinking, he was a psycho, why would anyone hurt animals??? I know saying this may be wrong but at that time this is what I was thinking, he was nuts!!! I dare not speak out if I said anything he doesn't like, I knew what would happen, he thought it was funny, I didn't, I'm scared of him. He was always saying he could and would kill, he seemed so proud of it, the times during beatings he would put his hand or elbow across my throat, I would be begging him to stop, I had repeatedly said sorry, sorry, sorry and he would stop. I would cry, but he blamed me for his actions, always saying it was my fault. I made him into a woman beater, and I should be grateful, as he saved me, as no-one loved or cared for me.

I spoke to his cousin the day we went shopping, she told me she hated the way he spoke to me in front of her and her family. I told her, not all of it, I didn't had time, I said he hits me and accuses me of affairs, I told her I'm unable to speak to my sister, Kim. She said if I need to speak to her, she would help, but guess what as soon as I got back, he started on me. It was the normal, he started again with me having affairs, I was a cunt, I treated him as a cunt, I was as lag a slut, a fucking user, then the liquids again, he threw coke over me, water, alcohol and that fish sauce, then to top it off he emptied a full ashtray over my head. I was trying to hold the tears back, because, yes, he would shout at me to stop crying. I sat on the bed, freezing. I was saying sorry, I wanted it to stop, my body and mind couldn't take it, no more. I started to shiver, after an hour he let me go and shower and I had twenty minutes. I showered trying to get the smell off me, of coke, fish sauce, the ashtray. I was as quick as I could be, I was running out of clothes. This happened daily, I had to clean up the mess, as I do all the time; he made it and I had to clean it up, and once again I didn't see his cousin again. He was moaning at me, saying I was getting on with her. He didn't trust me or her, I didn't see her again. I wanted to die, those feelings of wanting to die were daily, I just wanted this all to stop, my body aches and my mind felt nothing, I wanted peace. I would take an overdose, I had no medication as he stopped me from going to the doctor's. I hadn't had my medication for three months not since he found the phone number in my makeup, otherwise I would take them all and all of this would be over, peace at last, you see.

The last three months of him tying me up, the beatings and the mental abuse got worse, that was the last time I spoke to my sister, Kim. He had set up my Facebook behind my back on his computer and messaged all these men, until my sister rang, which I didn't knew as he always had the phone with him. He had turned the phone off, as soon as he turned it back on there were texts and missed calls from my sister. We were just getting in the car to visit his mum, I had been given my orders to smile and act normal. Kim had sent a text saying, "I had tried calling you, if you didn't ring me, I'm going to ring the police." He made me rang her, he wanted to know why she was sending texts like that; I said to him I didn't know, maybe it was because she couldn't get in touch. I rang her, Kim could sense something in my voice, maybe it was a sister thing, she knew something was wrong, but the thing was he always sat next to me if I received phone calls from my sister and friends, listening to our conversation. Kim said,

"I'm on loud speaker or you."

I replied, "No."

She said, "He was next to you."

I replied casually, "Oh, yeah."

She knows I couldn't talk openly, she then began to tell me my Facebook had been activated, she knows I closed it down. She said there were things on there that were not nice and he had messaged all these men, my sister had messaged them all to say it wasn't me. She also let family and friends knew it wasn't me, I answered Kim, "Oh, really, I didn't knew that." I was trying to act normal so he didn't suspect anything. She had reported it to Facebook to say it wasn't me. The thing was, I was forbidden to tell anyone exactly where I was, only that I'm in Dagenham, no one knows that I am on Greenlane. We pull up at his mum's, I said I had to go. She said to ring her when I could. As soon as I was off the phone, I was hit with questions, what did she want, what was she saying. He wanted to know everything, I had to come up with something quick. I said her son, Sam, and his girlfriend were sorting things out, I said Kim is a mum and just needed to chat, God, I hoped he believes it, otherwise he would start. He did believed me. In we go to his mum's, the false smile was on my face, and I had to act like everything was great, but inside I felt like I was dying, I felt nothing. You see, when you're told everyday how worthless, useless, you are, that no-one in your family loves you, that my mum and dad would be ashamed of me, that your ex-husband never loved you, I was adopted, that I'm nothing, he said evil things to me, I was a slut who would shag anyone, that no-one would care if I was here or not. You believed it, I did believed it, I believed no-one cared or loved me anymore so what was the point of living? If I was dead, I could be at peace, no more beatings, no more abuse.

On that day of my birthday, the day he tied me up, my sister, Kim, had sent me a text, as we were supposed to visit her on a few occasions, but obviously we didn't go as usual I had bruises. He knew we were supposed to go but he always started on me, how could I turn up with bruising? He would say, Kim sees you like that she wouldn't let you go, as I had lost more weight too. Kim sent a text. *You know, my aunt who was my dad's sister died with no specific reasons.* Kim said she was worried that it would happen to me. As I saw the text pinged on the phone, I read it trying to delete it because I knew if he saw that, he would start but I wasn't quick enough. He saw it and demanded to know why she had send a text like that, demanded to know why she had said that, had I said anything to her. I said no I hadn't, she was just being the older sister, but he didn't believed me. He kept on all evening, I wasn't going to break, I knew a beating would be next, I denied anything else; than what I had said, he stopped eventually, that was it, he changed the sim for the fourth time, this time, Kim's number was not on there. I thought that was it I had no one, it was just me and him. I was breaking inside, I was on my own and felt such alone.

Things got worse, I was walking on egg shells; it doesn't matter what I do from making a coffee, making food, to my driving. He criticised everything I do, how I dressed, he now picked my clothes. I had received payment from my ex-husband, I ended up with 26 thousand pounds, after I paid half of the court payment and what my ex lent me due to James making me text him for money. I was not allowed on his computer, and four days before I received this, he cut my bank card up, he gave me three chances as I answered him back but he cut my card up on my second chance. I started to cry, this was for me to find a way out, not now after what he had done, he turned to me and said, you would leave me that was why I did it. He told me to transfer all the money into his account, I refused, I didn't care if he beat me, I was not doing it. The next minute he took the baby and schools photos, the only ones I had of my daughters, the little proof, ones over the years I had kept them in my purse. He took them out and set fire to them, that killed me, it was all I had left of my daughters. I was heartbroken, I hated him!!! I hated him!! Why would he do this? He started to spend my money, I was not allowed to interfere, he bought everything, clothes, shoes, cars, everything he wanted.

I asked him one night, as he had set up eBay and PayPal in my name using my bank card that he had kept after cutting it up; why I knew this as he was having a bath, I risked looking around, putting everything back in place I found bits of my card under the keyboard. I dare not look around anymore in case he catches me. I was supposed to be grateful when he hands me clothes, and said look what I brought you. I just said, thank you, I couldn't keep this up, I had had enough, I just wanted peace to be dead. What happened when I asked him to delete eBay and PayPal, I got nothing but abuse, he told me to shut the fuck up, how dare I questioned him, if I questioned him once more, he would kill me. He said, and as I say, not as I do, he deserved to be treated like a king. You see, I didn't knew how degraded he was sexually, he abused my body, he hurt me, he wanted to doom me, do what he wanted to be pleasured by lots of women with me watching, that was not my thing. Never had been I knew, everybody had their own sexual desires or preferences, to be part of that was not my thing. I told him that, he went mad, I could see the anger in his eyes, the veins in his neck, he was spitting literally all because I said no, he told me he didn't care what I wanted, it was what he wanted and deserved. The next minute he said we were going out, out where, its 5:30 in the morning. Yes, he would go on at me all night, about what he deserved and wanted. I had to show remorse and affection to what he wanted, I didn't had the energy to refuse I knew he would keep going on with verbal abuse. We were in the car heading towards Ilford, I remembered this road, he had taken me along here once before, late at night, it was not until I see the sign from the police that crawlers would be prosecuted. I knew what was happening, the next minute he was out of the car, approaching a prostitute, the next, she was in the car, she introduced herself as Crystal. A few streets later we pull up in the road, I didn't knew the road or what was it called, he got out standing at the driver's door which was fully opened, she sat on the driver's seat. He had paid 25 pounds for a blow job, without a condom. He also told her, I had never done this; she was to teach me, she started to explain. I was not listening, all I did was to look out of the window, I could sense she was not impressed with him as he was trying to force her head more forward; as the next minute she was telling him not to do that, she would do it her way. He asked me if I was watching, I replied yes, but I was not, I was just staring out of the window. He couldn't see me as I was in the passenger seat, he asked her before if she swallowed, she said yes, but she didn't she spited it out on the pavement and road; he was not happy, I felt nothing inside, nothing at all. Afterwards it was just me and him in the car, he was moaning about her, she said she would swallow, she said I could force her head more, he didn't stop moaning, next minute we were back on Ilford road. He got out of the car and approached another prostitute. He took her number; she was a bit younger than the previous one. I was not judging what they did, you didn't know the reasons for doing it, like I always said you shouldn't judge a book by its cover. By the time we got back to the room, he was still moaning and said he felt dirty, he washed himself. I found him totally repulsive, I didn't wanted him anywhere near me, I stopped having sex with him for the last few months, I didn't wanted him even touching me, I couldn't stand him near me what so ever, like always he was blaming her and all women saying they were all sluts and slags, I didn't said anything. I was tired, exhausted, I hadn't spoken to anyone in three months, I think my body was giving up. He started on me again saying I never talked to him or started a conversation, that I stopped having sex. I told him he could go and be with anyone he wanted, I would not stop him, I pleaded with him to let me leave, I had pleaded with him many times to let me go. He would say yes, I was to go as I were, if I left he would push me down the stairs and tell people I done it myself; I had no choice but to stay. I started to cry, he told me to get on the bed, stay there and go to sleep; I wasn't to move, I was sobbing, I couldn't stop, he told me to shut the fuck up; I must had drifted off to sleep.

In the morning I woke up, he demanded a coffee, I made him one. I noticed he was done washing but he had put my clothes to one side, only was washing his. I asked him why, bloody hell, the next minute he had got me on the bed, his elbow digging into my throat, telling me to admit I had slept with all these men; that I was a slut and slag. I couldn't breathe, I was trying to get the words out; yes, yes, I'm sorry, I'm sorry. Next he was off me, I banged my head from the force off him pushing me on the bed, my forehead felt sore; God, that was close, he nearly killed me. I started crying the next on my knees, begging for my life, pleading with him not to kill me, I was sobbing even writing this, I had tears in my eyes. He told me he wouldn't if I showed him, how I was remorseful and sorry for treating him like a cunt. The next minute he was on his hands and knees saying, please forgive me, I know I had done you wrong, I know I had treated you bad, I was not worthy of you, I loved you so much; next he was standing and said that was what you had to do, ask for my forgiveness, for the way you had treated me. I was thinking I had lost it, my God, I was going to die, I didn't said anything, I was so scared. Now I knew he was capable of killing, he demanded food, I make him some and coffee. He was moaning because we had no ciggies, it was my fault. I went to say something, next he launched the phone at the television, it broke, there was no picture, it smashed it, and it was my fault; he ordered the telly on eBay, it was brand new, now the screen was in pieces, it was all my fault. He wanted a fag so I offered to go out and pick up dogends for him, yes, this is what I had to do, he was always with me, desperate for a ciggie, we would go out late at night picking up dogends so he could smoke. Yes, I smoked too but I could go longer without a ciggy.

I thought this was it, this was my chance to get out, my heart was beating fast, I mustn't show my feelings, show nothing about him letting me out, if he sensed anything, he wouldn't let me go. I acted normal, I said I would go, I wouldn't be long. To my relief he said yes, you got ten-minutes. *Bloody hell this is it, my glimmer of hope, stay calm, stay calm*; so I gave him a kiss on the cheek and said I wouldn't be long, I took the spare keys that he allowed me to had, he kept them so I don't run, I couldn't I had no energy, or strength. I tried looking over my shoulder I couldn't see anything, you see, he broke my glasses hours before because I didn't look at him when he asked me a question and he snapped them in half. I was trying to hurry, I couldn't, I was trying to look back I couldn't see far enough; I knew where I was going, to the doctors that he stopped me going too, minutes seemed like hours, he gave ten-minutes then he would come and see where I was. I was trying to walk fast if he caught me, he had dragged me back. I knew he would kill me. I made it, I was at the receptionist, I just asked for help, help me, I had got away from my abusive partner, please, help me, he would come looking for please help, I had lost control.

I was sobbing, they put me in a side and ring the police. In minutes the police were there, I broke down; I controlled my sobs, they were asking me to calm down as I had asthma, I hadn't had my inhalers for three months. I told them everything, the beatings, the mental abuse that he forced me to watch him with the prostitute, he said all the time if I left him, he would kill me, make his life worth finding me to kill me and my daughters. The doctor there recognised me, said I had been to see her. I was safe, I was crying; I was safe. The police wrote everything down, they took me to Barking police station in ariot and as I sit in the back, I couldn't believe I did it, I escaped. Tears in my eyes as I go over what happened that morning and afternoon.

They were so nice to me, and kind, they spoke to their inspector. For my own safety they need me out of London because of his threats to kill me and my daughters, they asked me if there is anyone I could ring. I said my sister, Kim, but because of him I didn't knew how she would say as he stopped our contact. So they let me ring a member of family whose house number I remembered, they gave me Kim's number. I heard her voice and started crying; I was asking if I could come to her, she said yes, but why hadn't I rang, I told her he got rid of your number. The police to talk to Kim explaining it was their duty to make me safe, they would be driving to Banbury for safety. Before we left, they asked me when was the last time I ate. I told them I think it was three days, they offered to buy me chips, but my stomach was in knots. They said you had to eat only if it was a little, I said yes, but it was a drink I needed so they got me a can of pop, I virtually drank it in one. I was so thirsty, and I ate a few chips before I knew it, I was in the police car and be driven home. I was nervous,

I didn't knew what Kim would think when she sees me, I was so thin, you could see my bones, I was not that curvy woman I once were; I was not Dana I once were. We arrived in Banbury at my sister's at 12:30 am on the 29th of May. I knocked the door, Kim answered it, we went into the living room, they spoke to Kim and explain some of what had happened and I would be hearing from them very soon. Just before they left, I couldn't thank them enough, I also gave them the spare keys to the room I shared with him.

As I sat down with Kim, she couldn't believe her eyes, I had bruises on my head, my chest and legs, no glasses, there was nothing left of me. She asked why I hadn't rang, I told her through sobs that he got rid of her number, I lost touch with everyone. She said she would arrange everything in the morning. She lent me a nightie which drowned me, but all I had was the clothes I was standing in, she said I was to sleep in Nathan's bed as he was on nights. I was tired, my body ached and hurt, I went to bed thinking how would the boys react to me and the rest of the family, my friends, before I knew, I must fell asleep.

Next Nathan was waking me up, I started crying he said it was alright you're safe. I headed downstairs, Kim had made me appointments to the Doctor, Opticians, and Social. The doctor first, I couldn't stop looking around, I was looking for him, I hadn't heard from the police yet as they took Kim's number as I had no phone. I told the doctor what had happened to me through crying, he put me on the sick, weighed me, I was 66 kilo's, he prescribes me drink supplements, because I had starved over the time in London, he also put me on antidepressants. I thanked him and he said he wanted to see me in a couple of weeks. Next it had the opticians, they order me new glasses. Then to Social, they couldn't do enough, Kim helped to explain what I had been through, because I didn't spoke to anyone. I found it hard to communicate, and explain as I couldn't get the words out, they set me up new details as he was able to access my account, I also closed my bank account, advised from the police as he knew my account number, he knew everything about me, my life because I trusted him from the beginning. That evening at Kim's the police rang and spoke to me, they explained that they went to arrest him but he wasn't there, they had been there a few times so they are looking for him. In the meantime a Detective Constable from the met in Essex rang me, she was in charge of the abuse unit in that area and wanted to visit to get statements from myself and Kim; they arrange a date, Kim had to take a photo of me and send it via email to the police for the case file.

Kim took me shopping, she wanted the clothes I wore in the bin; Nathan lent me a t-shirt and a pairs of his pants as all I was wearing was jeans, t-shirt and Ugg boots with a thin jacket. She was great she bought me clothes, underwear, shoes, make up, everything. I was a size 12, I had never been this size in my life ever. I felt clean, I showered, I was overwhelmed with everything I just kept breaking down; it was on the grapevine. I was back, my best friend, Lisa Manley, had been told, she messaged Kim on messenger and asked is it was true. Kim told her, yes, she was here safe; she asked Kim could she ring as I had no phone, she did. I couldn't believe I was hearing Lisa's voice, we both started crying, she was over the moon, I was safe. She told me outright, I thought you were dead, I had been trying to ring you. I told her, he changed the sim, I lost contact with everyone. She wanted me to visit when I was ready, so nice to hear her voice, no judgement just so happy to hear my voice. I also got in touch with Lydia, who was shocked to hear from me, again I'm crying explaining everything, she told me I was safe to come around when I was ready. I hadn't heard from the police yet either, so rang and asked I had the case number; I didn't had to explain everything they told me, not yet they hadn't found him. I was so scared, all the times he said he would find me if I left him, and kill me. I didn't go out on my own, I was with Kim or my Nephews, Nathan and Josh. I was so vigilant of whose around, I couldn't sit still, I was up and down, I was always checking at night to make sure everything was locked; I must drove everyone mad, but they totally understood. To eat again, like foods I had not eaten in months, it tasted good to eat cheese, tomatoes, cucumber; I mean this to me was lush, I couldn't stop eating. God, I made myself sick!! Kim had heard me and asked if I was okay,I replied it must had been the pot noodle; she started to laugh, not the chocolate, crisps, meat and everything else lol, I smiled, it had been months since I smiled. Kim also paid for my id, *she's fantastic*; she said he was trying to look like I was non-existence and I said to her, I nearly was.

The phone goes very late at night, Kim answered it. It was the police, they asked to speak to me, they told me he was been arrested. I started crying, they got him. He would now be interviewed by the Detective Constable from Essex; she rang me the next day as she kept me updated. I called the bank that I closed the account with on the advice of the police, they were so helpful after I explained everything, every phone call I made I had to explain, I always broke down. They sent me the statements, it proved the money he took and controlled of my account. The Detective Constable rang me and said they had interviewed him; could I send statements and asked for the doctor's statement as they needed to be sent all the relevant information to the Crown Prosecution Service; which I did as much as I could with the help of my sister, Kim, Nathan and Josh. The phone rang, the CPS is charging him with cohesive control and assault by beating, the DC rang to arrange a date to visit with her Detective Sergeant; I got to meet her after three months of talking on the phone. She reassured me so much, I was scared of what he might do, I was nervous meeting her but when she arrived, she and her DS, made me and my sister, Kim, feel so relaxed. I gave statements, God, so much happened to me by his hands; I cried a lot while giving my statement, they were fantastic. The DS took a statement from my sister; I knew Kim found it very hard too. As my friend, Lisa, was the last of my friends to talk to me they wanted a statement from her. I rang her to ask if she could come and see her, Lisa said yes, straight away. They also needed to visit my doctor surgeon; DC kept me updated.

As the weeks went by, I was having nightmares at night. I knew how lucky I was to be here but it was not how my mind saw it, I always kept thinking what would had happened if I hadn't escaped; that what was in my mind daily. If I heard a loud sound of a car, I would be up at the window, if I didn't recognised cars, I questioned whose it was, I would keep checking the doors, windows, I couldn't help it. During this time I received great support from Headway, as I suffered a brain hemorrhage when I was 25,I was also expecting my first daughter, but I refused treatment as I wanted my baby. I had my daughter three weeks early by c-section, awake too; five weeks later I was in the Hallamshire Hospital in Sheffield having laser treatment. After two and a half years I was given the all clear, but I noticed my memory had been effected by what had happened to me, which the doctor, my neurosurgeon, confirmed, even when I fell pregnant with my second daughter I still had to had a c-section, my sister noticed my memory was terribly worse than ever. I had trouble and still do, talking and getting the words out, because he hit so many times around my head. I swear he had done some damage; I just come out to Kim what he did to me which was hard to say, I cried a lot, but Headway support was amazing. I felt they understood, it just seemed all this support had come at once, I had Nikki, my counsellor, then I meet Ellie, my cognitive behaviour therapist visits, she explained everything what she would help with; I broke down because some of what he did I feel ashamed off. Our sessions started, my God, it was hard I cried a lot, but she was with every step of the way; she explained I suffer with post-traumatic stress disorder, and what I had been through was traumatic. It was my brain's way of dealing with any situation that reminded me of what happened to me; it kind of shuts off that how my brain dealt with it. I couldn't deal with too much information, I couldn't progress it, I looked to Kim a lot to help explain to me in my terms so I understand better. I noticed changes in my body, I ached all the time, I kept falling asleep a lot, one minute I was talking to Kim or the boys, the next I was asleep. Kim made an appointment, I got to see him anyway, both my hands were suffering with pins and needles, especially the right, it was painful. I went to the doctor, Kim was with me because I found it hard to explain sometimes and I could drift off talking about something else. I had blood tests and he sent me to had my pulses done in my wrists. I went for my appointment, I got a phone call about my blood test I got in a couple of days later. I had less than 30% of vitamin D in my body, I didn't knew how serious it was, I suffered with fatigue too. I had to take 1,000 units of vitamin D every three days for five weeks, folic acid too for longer, but I had to take vitamin D for the rest of my life. I had carpool tunnel severely bad in my right wrist and it was not great in my left; I had an injection to help with the pain, which it did. I also had a lump on the top right of my breastbone, I went for a mammogram and ultra sound. I explained to them what I had been through, it was cartilage; due to the violence, he always sat across my chest with his knees digging in, I always had bruising across my chest. My GP told me my body had been through so much, it would take a very long time to recover; my mind would take even longer. I now knew why my body felt like this daily. Doing simple tasks was hard for me, my posture was so bad as I walked with my head down and my shoulders; I ended up going to physio to help with it. I found it hard as I was so tired all the time, when I had to go out with him, I always walked behind him with my head down; he would accuse me of not wanting to walk with him but as thin as I got, I had no strength or energy.

I got a phone call from my other sister, Glenda. She told me he had put on his Facebook, he was in Banbury showing a map. I started to panic, I rang the witness centre to tell; they advised me to be aware and ring 999 if I see him. Nathan was with me, I knew he wouldn't let anything happen to me, because he was told he was not allowed to come near me, my family or Banbury, directly or indirectly. Next minute my phone rang, yes, after nearly four months of being in a safe house, I got myself a phone, pay as you go, no contract, a phone I brought from a supermarket. It was DC, she was rung by the witness unit, I told her what my sister told me, because he was due to go before the court on the 28th August 2018, this was a few days before he had to do his plea. She reassured me, I got back to Kim as I was so nervous and scared; the comfort from my family was fantastic. A couple of days later I got a phone call from the witness unit that said he was absconded, he didn't turn up to court, so they had put a warrant out for his arrest, Jesus Christ this was not the news I wanted, I was scared even more now because he always said he would find me and kill me. When I first escaped my sister's house was my safe house, it was linked to the police as well as our phones. I was asked if I wanted one of the panic phones, my phone would do the same job ring 999, give my location so I if stuck with my phone, I was never on my own, even more. So now, I was even worse at night, I kept checking everything was secured, my nightmares became worse. He was always running after me, I kept running but I would always woke up. Kim would say to me in the mornings that she could hear me shouting out no, no, no. I told her my nightmares she knew I was having them, I had to inform my support workers because he had done a runner, so all of my sessions were done over the phone. I completely understood why, because of the risk to them, they must feel safe too. My family was brilliant, they knew how I was feeling and kept my chin up; I even started to smile because Nathan and Josh had me in stiches. Their dog, Bracken, I loved her; she become a great comfort to me. It had been a long time since I laughed, but I knew that I had changed inside, which I told my CBT lady; I used to be so affectionate and loving, I felt I had lost these. She reassured me it was my brain reacting to what had happened and they would come back eventually; I found it hard to express love.

I had a social worker who puts me forward to go on a course for victims of domestic violence and abuse, I agreed and I got a phone call from them telling me what time and day; it was called the Freedom Course. I couldn't tell you anything else as it still runs for other victims that are sometimes still in the relationship. It was my first week, God, I was so nervous, I had a car now that we brought of my great friend, Lydia. I had to go on my own, I was seriously thinking of backing out, I always had someone with me, but Kim encouraged me to go, told me to text her when I was there. I drove there, doors locked; I went into the building, I was met by two ladies. I sat there waiting as we all go up together; I was so nervous, I hardly spoke. We got into the room then it began; I introduced myself as does everyone else. I was very quiet as I didn't knew these people but they asked if I wanted to speak, I plucked up the courage too, then I started telling them how I escaped, it just came rolling off my tongue. I was sobbing; the other ladies were taken out of the room. I was left with one of the counsellors who comforted and chatted to me, I had calmed down; God knows what the others thought but they were so kind and understood exactly what I had been through. Meeting these brave ladies who had welcomed me, had touched me so much. Every week I went to the course I cried, every week, until I could speak without crying because they gave me the strength to. I kept them updated on everything they were so supportive.

I then received information from DC that another unit had taken over of finding him as they would be on the case 24/7. I was very aware of my surroundings, never on my own. I finished the course with these brave and courageous women, I got a certificate, I was really proud of myself. I was realising a little that this wasn't my fault; I didn't deserved to be treated in that way. I wanted to know why? Why he had treated me this way, what gave him the right to? I tried and carried on as normal especially with him. Still on the run, my nephews were protective and Kim as always. I was in touch with the met police, they updated me with any news so far there was none. I got a phone call from my sister, she told me she had found him on Facebook, in a relationship with another woman in Bedfordshire. I rang the local police who transferred me to the Bedfordshire police but I was unable to get through so I was then transferred to the met police; I explained everything, they had my case number, they passed the information to the unit who were looking for him. I received a phone call saying that the police had been to this woman's address, he was gone!!! The met police reassured me, they would find him and they did a couple of days later, back in London; he was arrested, charged and bailed!! Detective Constable rang me and said she wanted him in custody, no one had dealt with the paperwork; the magistrate gave bail with very strict conditions. The DC also went to his address unannounced and made it very clear to him if he absconds again, he would be in trouble. I cried when they rang and said they got him, I sobbed a lot and I rang family and friends, Lisa and Lydia, and told them. The witness service rang me, Kim and Lisa with a date for the trial, Monday 4th of November 2019, they asked if we were on holiday, hospital appointments, I said no.

This was in September, it seemed a long way off but it came around quick. Prior to the trial the witness service appointed support, his name was Derek, he was kind, and explained everything. We were taken to Oxford Crown Court to had a look around, as I had never been in a court, Kim, Lisa and myself were giving a video link from Oxford to London. This was it, the first day of the trial. I was not feeling nervous, I couldn't understand why? We were given our statements to refresh our memories, what he did to me would stay with me forever. I was learning to put these memories further back inside my head, it was 2 pm, I walking to the link room with Derek to start my evidence. I sat upright and I looked straight into the camera; I knew he could see me but I couldn't see him, I didn't wanted to see him. I started to give evidence, the prosecutor asked me questions and I answered every one as hard and emotional as it was. I was determined to fight him all the way; it was very emotional. I broke down crying serval times, the judge stopped it to give me a few minutes to recover, I gave more evidence until 4 pm. The first day was finished, I was tired and we traveled back. By the time we got home, it was 7 pm, totally shattered. We tried watching something on telly which was light hearted. Tuesday, we were back in court for 10 am. I was back in the link room with Derek, he was brilliant; just knowing he was sat there that was reassuring for me. I continued to give evidence, what I had written in this book was what I was telling the court; the mental abuse went on for hours, he would never stop. It was more emotional, I broke down again and again. The judge was very understanding and we stopped and had a drink, and for myself to recover; my evidence was over. I also had bank statements of the amount of money he took, also his Aunt gave evidence against him. Then I was cross examined by his defense, he asked me the same question but in different ways and my answer was the same; the judge even stopped him to tell him to move on. I was cross examined for four hours, then the judge told me I was released. We arrived in court on Wednesday, everyone had turned up: Judge, Jury, us but it was adjourned, as I was missing one page of evidence from my bank statements. We traveled to Northampton to get what was needed, once I found where the bank was, I explained everything; they were more than happy to help. They gave me what was needed with no charge, and I let the DC know. I forwarded those by email for the prosecutor, Kim and Lisa gave there evidence and were questioned on Thursday and Friday. The trial would continue in London on Monday.

I got a phone call on Wednesday 13th of November, it was the afternoon, as my sister, Kim, and I were picking up Nathan from work, it was the Detective Constable, asking me the full names of my daughter's, I told. I looked at Kim, we both started to chat, the Jury was out, it was just awaiting game, Nathan was out, we go the long way around, it seemed to be busy that day, coming down the Warwick Road, my phone rang, Kim answered it and put it on loud speaker; it was the Detective. She asks if I was alright, I answered I was okay, I stopped the car on the main road, there was a few minutes of silence, the next thing she was saying, he had been found 'guilty'!!! Unanimously, 'guilty' of cohesive of control, 'guilty' of assault by beating. I started sobbing, real sobbing, she was asking are they tears of joy, I said, absolutely, 'yes'!!! I didn't realised I was causing traffic jam; Nathan told to park around the corner. I was so relieved, so many emotions were inside of me, Kim and Nathan were comforting me; DC told me she would ring me later. I was still in shock. I was just overwhelmed, we got back home, we told Josh and Jess, I rang Lisa, Lydia and my sister Glenda. He got 3 years in prison; I was still in a daze. The door-bell rang, it was about 5 o'clock, standing there was DC; I started crying. We were just stood there hugging, I couldn't thanked her enough; she came in, Kim thanked her so do Josh and Nathan. She said I did so brilliant, as hard as it was to hear everything said in court, she was proud of me. She said the evidence was so much, I didn't knew when I escaped to the doctor's, they had cameras; DC said I looked disheveled, thin, bruised, and sobbing, shaking. She said to look at me now, then to look at me then, it was like two different women. I thanked her and her team for everything they had done, amazing!!! I was so happy, he was now in prison; 'justice' for me, protection for other women from him, this was it; the beginning of my new life!!!

All the support I had had, my family, friends and Headway, Counsellors, my support network were so amazing. I could now look forward; I couldn't and wouldn't let him control my life no more!!! This was a new beginning, even now I still had counselling, months after the verdict. Yes, I suffered from mental health, anxiety, depression and fatigue; it took its toll on me. I was getting stronger every day, my life had changed completely; counselling helped so much. I was learning to live again, be happy in myself. I was in my new flat, my choices, my decisions, and it was secure, my family and friends were fantastic; my nephews: Nathan, Josh, Daniel and Jess helped in getting my flat ready for me to move into because I value my privacy and security. They rang me every day to make sure I was okay. I visited my family and friends, they visited me, I had my independence. I would never ever forget what he did to me, it would stay with me for the rest of my life; it had changed me. It was trust I still struggle with, to think where I was 2 years ago, to where I was now, I never thought my life would be like this, ever. I had written this book to let people know it was real, it happened, if I could help just one person to make the decision to escape, I'm happy. I hope this gives men and women hope, strength, courage and eventually a new life. When I was ready I wanted to train as a counsellor, I wanted to help others like me, and I just need to thank my sister, Kim; my nephews: Sam, Josh, Nathan, Daniel and Jess; my friends: Lisa, Lydia, Andrea and Jane, thank you so much for saving me, supporting me and being there for me through everything. Thank you!!!

CPSIA information can be obtained
at www.ICGtesting.com
Printed in the USA
LVHW020416221122
733727LV00029B/729

9 781398 424715